Girls Love
Gymnastics

★ American Girl®

Published by American Girl Publishing, Inc.
Copyright © 2007 by American Girl, LLC

Questions or comments? Call 1-800-845-0005, visit our Web site at americangirl.com, or write to Customer Service, American Girl, 8400 Fairway Place, Middleton, WI 53562-0497.

Printed in China
07 08 09 10 11 12 13 LEO 10 9 8 7 6 5 4 3 2 1

Editorial Development: Sara Hunt, Carrie Anton
Art Direction and Design: Camela Decaire
Production: Mindy Rappe, Gretchen Krause, Jeannette Bailey, Judith Lary
Illustrations: Carol Yoshizumi
Photography: Radlund Studios, except as noted

Special thanks to Stacey Brickson, Ph.D., P.T., A.T.C.; Michelle Carhart; Charley Cotter; Sarah Nelson; Caroline Smith; and all the coaches and gymnasts at Madtown Twisters

Hair stylist, pp. 16–17, 20–21, and 23—Jemree Robinet; pp. 53, 55—Pam Retelle; Courtney D.—photos courtesy of the family; Sarah B.—photos courtesy of Marvin Moore; Hannah K.—photos courtesy of the family; Heather U.—professional photos courtesy of Stacey Champion, Champion Images, other photos courtesy of the family; Rebecca B.—photos courtesy of the family; poster photography—Fotosearch

Dear Reader,

This book covers the basics of each of the **four artistic gymnastics events.** Plus, five gymnasts share their stories of the twists and turns of participating—and competing—in gymnastics. Flip through the pages of **games, crafts,** and **hairdos** for girls who love gymnastics. We've even included some delicious and nutritious **recipes** to keep you feeling tip-top for tumbling.

Finally, in the back, score an **insider's guide** to gymnastics terms and five **fun posters** that are all about gymnastics!

If you like gymnastics, you'll **flip for the fun** in *Girls Love Gymnastics*!

Your friends at American Girl

Contents

Basics

True Stories

Gym Fun

Basics

Start smart with the basics—from bars to beam and stretching to safety.

Why Gymnastics?

Friends, fitness, and fun—you'll flip for gymnastics!

If you like to do running round-offs at recess or handstands outside your house, then gymnastics just might be the sport for you! Gymnastics combines fitness, fun, and friends while also challenging your body and your brain.

There are several types of gymnastics, including artistic, rhythmic, acrobatic, and trampoline and tumbling. Artistic is the most common and includes learning skills for four different events: vault, uneven bars, balance beam, and floor exercise.

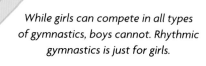

While girls can compete in all types of gymnastics, boys cannot. Rhythmic gymnastics is just for girls.

Whenever a posed leg is purposely bent, it is called a stag. *This pose is a single stag.*

Have What It Takes to Tumble?

Gymnastics is more than flipping and flopping and whirling and twirling. See if you're ready to jump into gymnastics.

Gymnasts must:
- enjoy being active.
- not be afraid to try new things.
- have a positive attitude.
- handle comments—good or bad—from coaches, as well as teammates.
- work well on a team.
- practice, practice, practice.

Getting Started

Stretch smart to make the most of your muscles.

The more flexible you are, the easier time you'll have as a gymnast. But even if you can't bend over and touch your toes, don't think that you can't cut it in gymnastics. Stretching your muscles every day will help you get loosened and limber in no time!

Most gymnastics practices begin or end—or both—with stretching all the major muscle groups: neck, shoulders, back, hips, and upper and lower legs. Be sure to warm up "cold" muscles before stretching by skipping or running around. Once you're warmed up, you're ready to stretch!

Simple Stretch to Try at Home

You don't have to be in the gym to focus on flexibility. Try doing some stretches while you're watching TV. Get started with the butterfly sit.

Sit on the floor with the bottoms of your feet together in front of you. Lean forward slowly until you feel a stretch in the inside of your upper legs. For more of a stretch, use your arms to gently push your knees to the floor (no bouncing).

Vault

Launching and landing could lead you to a perfect score.

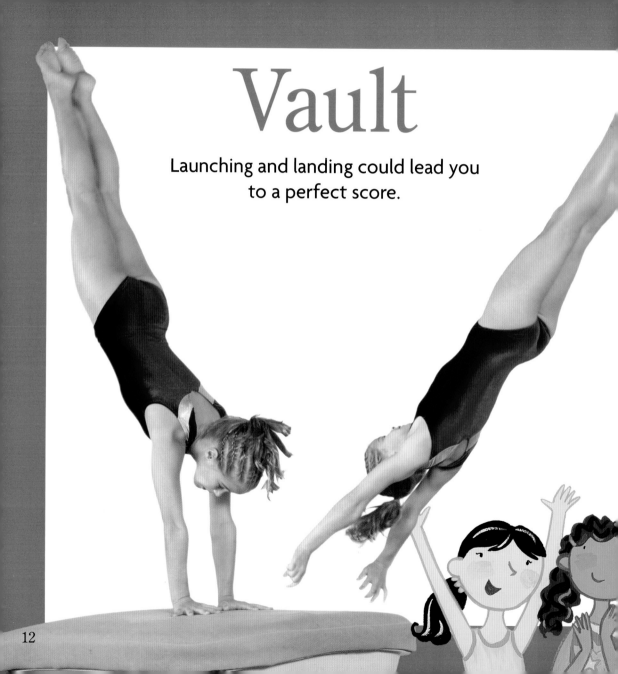

A strong vault starts out with a fast run before the gymnast explodes off a spring-board, uses her hands to push off from the vault table, and rotates in the air before land-ing. The runway leading to the springboard is usually about 80 feet long, which allows the gymnast to gain enough speed to complete her skill in the air. The saying "If at first you don't succeed, try, try again" seems fitting for the vault. It's the only event that allows gym-nasts two tries in competition—sometimes only the higher score counts, and other times an average of the two scores is used.

Gymnasts try not to take any steps on the dismount. This is called sticking *the landing.*

Uneven Bars

Get into the swing of things!

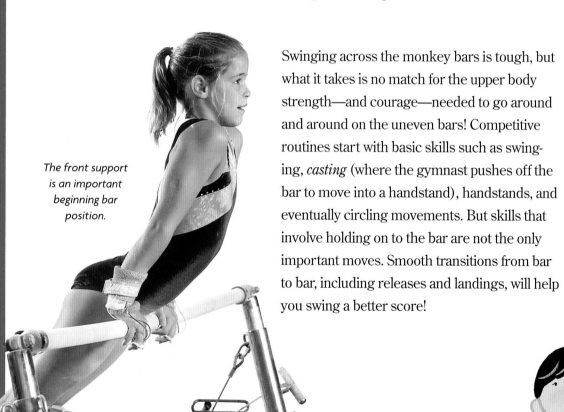

The front support is an important beginning bar position.

Swinging across the monkey bars is tough, but what it takes is no match for the upper body strength—and courage—needed to go around and around on the uneven bars! Competitive routines start with basic skills such as swinging, *casting* (where the gymnast pushes off the bar to move into a handstand), handstands, and eventually circling movements. But skills that involve holding on to the bar are not the only important moves. Smooth transitions from bar to bar, including releases and landings, will help you swing a better score!

Get a Grip

Swinging on the bars can be fun but also painful. To help prevent blisters and rips, gymnasts wear *grips*, or hand guards, which fit over the middle fingers and secure around the wrist with VELCRO® closures or buckles. Gymnasts also rub chalk on their hands and grips to soak up sweat and keep their hands from slipping.

Before a gymnast can begin circling movements, she must first be able to do a handstand on the bar.

15

Balance Beam

On hands or on feet, balance is the key to being best on beam.

If you can stand on one foot without a lot of wiggling, then the balance beam just might be your thing. A balance beam stands 4 feet off the ground but is only 4 inches wide. On this very small space, gymnasts spin, tumble, leap, and pose—and all without wobbling. A wobble might lead to a lower score or even cause a gymnast to fall to the floor.

To maintain balance, keep your head up while focusing on the end of the beam.

Practice Makes Perfect

You don't need an actual beam to practice a routine. Put a 4-inch-wide and 16-foot-long piece of masking tape on your floor or carpet. Using the moves below, make up your own balance beam routine. Use a stopwatch or timer to try to keep your routine under 60 seconds—the average length of a competitive routine.

V-sit   passé (pah-say)   arabesque

Floor Exercise

Tumbling and dance are paired with music
for this fun event.

The floor exercise combines high-flying tumbling with graceful dance moves and is the only artistic gymnastics event that is choreographed to music. Routines are between 60 and 90 seconds long and are performed on a bouncy carpeted floor made to help gymnasts jump higher and land softer. Floor routines are scored not just on the moves the gymnast makes but also on how much floor space is used—the more the better!

*Pointed toes, good
form, and strong
dance technique are
as important to a floor
routine as tumbling.*

Tumble Tips

Gymnasts build on basic skills, such as cartwheels and handstands, to learn more difficult skills such as flips, handsprings, and aerials. Try to master this move, then put it to music!

Cartwheel step-by-step

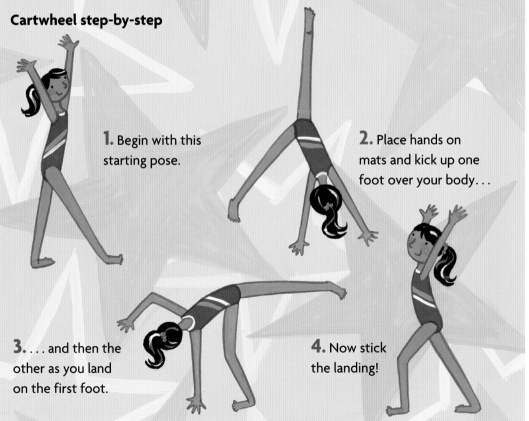

1. Begin with this starting pose.

2. Place hands on mats and kick up one foot over your body...

3. ... and then the other as you land on the first foot.

4. Now stick the landing!

Meet Time

After months of practice, competitions are gymnasts' time to shine!

The reason some gymnasts decide to dedicate so much of their personal time to practicing—aside from having fun and getting good exercise—is competitions, or "meets." Let's take an insider's look at meets, from points won (and lost) to what to wear and what to do.

Individual scores for each event are determined by taking either the average of scores from multiple judges, or the score assigned by a single judge when judging alone. A 10 is the highest possible individual event score.

The **all-around** score is the total score for the four events: vault, uneven bars, balance beam, and floor. The highest possible all-around score is 40. The best gymnasts are good on all events and place high in all-around.

Deductions

"Deductions," or losing points, happen when a gymnast uses poor form, steps out of bounds, or doesn't complete necessary skills. Falling off the apparatus can make the difference between earning a gold medal and getting no medal at all, but losing points isn't always about how you perform.

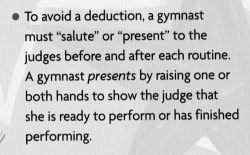

- To avoid a deduction, a gymnast must "salute" or "present" to the judges before and after each routine. A gymnast *presents* by raising one or both hands to show the judge that she is ready to perform or has finished performing.

- Beam and floor routines have time limits. A deduction is taken for going over the time limit, and some judges will not count skills performed after time is called.

- A big deduction is taken for floor routines with no music or with music that has words—instrumental music only, please!

Gear Up

Points also come into play when judging how a gymnast looks:

- While gymnasts usually wear sleeveless leotards, or "tanks," for practicing, competition leotards ("leos") must have long or three-quarter-length sleeves. These leos can be made from velour, spandex, or metallic fabric and must fit perfectly—gymnasts can lose points for adjusting their leos while performing.

- Gymnasts often wear underwear called "trunks" under their leos. Trunks must match the color of their leotards. If they don't, judges can take points away.

- A gymnast should keep her hair pulled back so that it doesn't get caught in equipment. Having loose hair or wearing jewelry, nail polish, or too much makeup—called "improper uniform"—can lead to lost points.

Level-Headed

A gymnast can begin competing at meets when she reaches Level 4. With each level, the gymnast may need to practice longer to learn new, more difficult skills. Some skills, such as split jumps and leaps, remain the same from level to level but require a higher degree of leg separation, making the skill harder to perform without error. Here's a look at skills required in each level:

Level	Vault	Bars	Beam	Floor
1–4	Drills not using the vault	Cast with straight body	Forward roll	Back walkover
		Pullover	Tuck jump	Half turn
		Back hip circle	Handstand	Split leap
5–6	Handspring	Kip	Cartwheel	Dive roll
		Clear hip circle	Split jump	Front tuck
		Flyaway dismount	Back walkover	Two front handsprings
7–8	Handspring (level 7) and open choice (level 8)	Giant	Salto dismount	Back salto layout
		Cast handstand	Full pirouette	Forward tumbling pass
		Uprise	Back handspring	Dance series

Safety

Minimize the aches and pains of practicing and competing.

Gymnastics requires a lot of practice and repetition. Repetitive training can leave gymnasts' muscles and joints sore, or even injured. Ouch! Flexibility and focusing on good technique are two ways to help lessen aches and pain, but injuries do happen even with the best precautions. Sprained wrists and ankles are common injuries, and either can cause swelling or bruising. Let your parent or coach know about an injury first so that she or he can determine if a doctor is needed.

Not stretching enough can lead to pulled muscles, but not being strong enough can cause more serious injuries.

Basic First-Aid Rules

Joints can get sore from performing the same skill hundreds of times. A doctor or coach might give you these tips to use in the first 24 to 48 hours to ease the pain. R.I.C.E. is an easy way to remember.

Rest. Limit the use of the injured area—for example, by using crutches when walking with a sore ankle.

Ice. Apply a towel-covered ice pack to help reduce swelling and ease pain. (Do not put ice directly on the skin.) It's recommended to ice the ankle for 20 minutes at a time every hour for several hours.

Compression. Have a coach or parent wrap the ankle with an elastic bandage to help minimize swelling.

Elevation. Keep the sprained ankle raised on a pillow to help reduce the swelling.

Courtney   age 10

Began gymnastics: age 5
Favorite food: mac 'n' cheese

Sarah   age 8

Began gymnastics: age 2
Favorite animal: horse

Hannah   age 12

Began gymnastics: age 2
Favorite book: *Soul Surfer*
by Bethany Hamilton

Rebecca   age 8

Began gymnastics: age 4
Favorite color: purple

Heather   age 8

Began gymnastics: age 4
Favorite movie: *Cheaper by the Dozen*

True Stories

Read the true stories of five real girls
who love gymnastics!

Courtney

Courtney D. strikes a balance between gymnastics goals and getting good grades.

Since starting gymnastics at age five, Courtney has learned that balance is just as important outside the gym as it is on the beam. "I've always remained on the honor roll while in gymnastics. I maintain my grades because, if I didn't, I wouldn't have a gymnastics story to tell," says Courtney. She claims gymnastics is her life but is quick to add that education comes first. Before the 16 hours of practice Courtney has each week, she finishes her homework at home or on the way to and from the gym. "I study so that I won't have to worry about school while I'm at gymnastics—or worry about gymnastics while I'm at school."

When she is in the gym, Courtney is focused on overcoming the challenges gymnasts face when moving up in levels. Just as someone

"I've learned a lot in this sport, but mostly gymnastics has taught me that I have to be disciplined and have tons of dedication."

has to master the times table before tackling long division in math, Courtney had to master her giant (a skill on bars) to move up from Level 6 to Level 7. "Giants were so difficult because I couldn't cast high enough, making it hard to swing all the way around," she remembers. But she didn't give up.

Courtney knew practice would eventually pay off for her bar routine, just as studying hard leads to good grades. "But when it was my turn one day at practice to do the giant without my coach, I had a big knot in my stomach. With my teammates there to cheer me on, I went for it." When she nailed the skill, Courtney knew that all the practice had been worth it. "After tons of hard work, dedication, sweat, and tears, I felt I had finally made it."

With her giant skill behind her, Courtney keeps practicing so that she can master the next set of challenges that come her way. "You have to be dedicated to the sport, because if your heart isn't in it, you won't get any better," says Courtney. "I've learned a lot in this sport, but mostly gymnastics

has taught me that I have to be disciplined and have tons of dedication." But most of all, Courtney has learned that she can accomplish almost anything—in or out of the gym—so long as she balances her time and keeps working hard.

Sarah

In rhythmic gymnastics, Sarah B. knows trying your best is more important than keeping your ball—or rope—in the air.

Sarah started out where most girls do, in artistic gymnastics, learning skills in the four different artistic events. But when she wasn't practicing vault, uneven bars, balance beam, and floor exercise, Sarah was drawn to watching the rhythmic gymnastics practices. At age five, Sarah decided it was time to trade in the balance beam and uneven bars for a rope and a ball.

Rhythmic gymnastics is a bit like ballet and a bit like artistic gymnastics. Imagine tossing a hoop in the air and catching it with your foot, or rolling a ball across your back from one fingertip to the other. Those are just two of the many tricks Sarah will have to master in this form of gymnastics.

In rhythmic gymnastics, you get to work *with* equipment instead of *on* equipment. Five kinds of equipment are used when competing: rope, hoop, ball, clubs, and ribbon. As a Level 4 gymnast, Sarah uses only the rope and the ball; still, she has all of the equipment so that she can work with her coach to start getting a feel for the other pieces before the time comes to move up. "I really like all the equipment, but I think ribbon is the prettiest to watch, with hoop coming in second," says Sarah. But rhythmic gymnastics is not only about the equipment; it's also about technique. A gymnast must focus on developing poise, posture, flexibility, strength, and presentation—all while keeping ribbons twirling and hoops spinning. It's not always that easy to do, as Sarah learned at a competition at which her rope twisted around itself. "I had to figure out how to keep the performance going even though the routine wasn't going well. I was hoping during some of the movements that the rope would untwist. But I just kept going and finished the routine."

During Sarah's first year competing, she made it to her state's regional championship, along with six other girls from her gym in the same level. For girls who didn't qualify for nationals during the season, this meet was the last chance to make it. At the awards ceremony, the national team for Sarah's level was announced and given flowers—all but Sarah had made the team. "I felt very sad that everyone was going to nationals and I wasn't," remembers Sarah.

Afterward, Sarah's teammates and the older girls from her gym offered hugs and encouragement. "They all tried to cheer me up," says Sarah, "and my coach made time to tell me that I did a great job." But the most meaningful response came from one of Sarah's teammates. "She came up to me to say how well I did and gave me her flower." Sarah put it in a water bottle and carried it in the car all the way from Florida to Tennessee!

Once Sarah decided not to be sad anymore, she knew it was time to return the favor and cheer her team on. She made cards for all the girls going to nationals and included personal notes wishing them luck at the meet. Sarah may not have made it to nationals this time, but she says, "No matter what happens, if you do your best, you can be very proud of yourself."

"No matter what happens, if you do your best, you can be very proud of yourself."

Rhythmic Equipment

Rope

The length of the rope depends on the size of the gymnast. Leaps and skipping are the basic parts of Sarah's routine, but she may also swing and throw the rope, or rotate it in circles and figure eights.

Hoop

The hoop is about three feet across and is made of wood or plastic. Sometimes the gymnast might leap through the hoop or toss it up and catch it behind her back. She may also roll and spin the hoop on the ground—or even on parts of her body!

Ribbon

The ribbon, about 15 feet long, is made of satin and attached to a stick. Holding the stick, the gymnast twirls the ribbon in figure eights, spirals, and snakes. The ribbon must always be in motion or the gymnast could lose competition points.

Clubs

There are two clubs, each of which is made of wood and looks like a long bottle. Throughout the routine the gymnast must use one or both hands to throw, catch, and make small circles with the clubs, among other skills.

Ball

The ball, used in one event Sarah competes in, is made of rubber or plastic and weighs less than a pound. Throughout her routine, Sarah can throw, bounce, or roll the ball, but she cannot grasp the ball or rest it on her wrist.

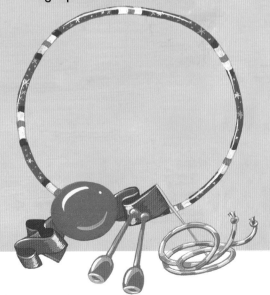

Hannah

Instead of a skill, Hannah K. struggles with her "HIPPO" to move up in levels.

Once a gymnast masters a skill, she has a whole new set of challenges to face as she moves on to the next, more difficult, skill. This was no different for Hannah, who has been a gymnast for more than nine years. But two years ago, when she wanted to move up from Level 6 to Level 7, it wasn't a front handspring or flyaway dismount that was giving her problems—instead, it was her back.

At the beginning of Hannah's Level 6 season, a gymnast on her team noticed a small lump on Hannah's lower back. After having it checked by a physical therapist, who thought it was just an enlarged muscle, Hannah was seen by an orthopedic surgeon, who took X-rays. "When I saw the X-rays,

I started crying, because my spine looked like an 's.'" says Hannah. It was then that Hannah was diagnosed with *scoliosis*, a condition in which the spine curves instead of

staying straight. People with scoliosis can sometimes have one curve, which is called a "c" curve, or, like Hannah, two curves, which is called an "s" curve. While some people's spines curve only a little bit, the curves in Hannah's spine were much worse.

"The doctor said I needed to start wearing a brace until I was finished growing, which would be in about five years," explains Hannah, who received her brace just ten days before her eleventh birthday. This was a birthday "present" she'd soon want to return. "The brace was horrible! The rigid plastic surrounded me from my armpits to my hips. It was extremely hot and gave me a heat rash, as well as made sores where it rubbed on my hips. I couldn't take deep breaths or even finish yawning."

Despite changing braces three times, the fit and comfort never got any better. Hannah soon started calling this uncomfortable contraption her "HIPPO," which stands for "Horrible Idiotic Pathetic Plastic Object." Hannah had to wear her HIPPO at all times, except when bathing or at the gym. "I did not let this stop me from doing gymnastics," says Hannah. "In fact, it made me work that much harder, because I wanted to be better than those gymnasts with straight backs!"

That year, Hannah moved up in levels, competing in two Level 7 meets before

"It made me work that much harder, because I wanted to be better than those gymnasts with straight backs!"

moving on to Level 8. In her fourth Level 8 meet—a state meet—Hannah placed third on the balance beam and fourth on the floor. She was even the first alternate for the Level 8 regional meet!

During the summer of 2006, Hannah underwent an experimental procedure so that she could ditch her HIPPO sooner than when she stops growing. She was hoping that she would never have to wear the brace once her surgery and healing time were complete, but her lower curve needed more correction, so the HIPPO is back on. But Hannah is grateful that she has to wear it only at home during the evenings and while she sleeps.

Hannah should be competing again by the winter—and can't wait! "Despite all of this, I continue to pursue my dream of being the best gymnast I can be."

Rebecca

Rebecca B. didn't let a "freeze" get the best of her and her high-flying goals.

Many people are afraid to fly. For gymnasts, a fear of flying sometimes has nothing to do with airplanes but instead involves the high-flying air stunts they perform. In artistic gymnastics, gymnasts can get pretty high on the vault, uneven bars, and even floor exercise, but for tumbling and trampoline gymnasts, skills rise to a whole new level—sometimes even as high as 30 feet!

Rebecca, a Level 6 tumbling and trampoline gymnast, competes on trampoline, on double mini-trampoline, and in power tumbling for her team. She joined this sport when she was two and hopes one day to compete at an elite level.

"It's weird because you know you are capable of doing the skill, but something in your brain just won't let you."

"Trampoline is my favorite, because it is fun to try new skills and keep trying to get higher and longer air times," says Rebecca. It's obvious that Rebecca has no problems with flying fears, but when it came time to practice a flip-flop on ground level to perform at her state meet—a skill she had done many times before—she froze. "All of a sudden I could not throw my flip-flops. I would do my round-off and just stop."

As Rebecca soon learned, a freeze can be very annoying. Many gymnasts have them and say it feels as if their brains don't know how to tell their bodies to do the tricks anymore. "I spent weeks getting more and more frustrated," explains Rebecca. "It's weird because you know you are capable of doing the skill, but something in your brain just won't let you."

Rebecca's coaches, mom, and teammates supported her through the tough time. They never gave up on her and wouldn't let her quit. After trying many different ways to help, Rebecca's coaches suggested she try the only place she could do this stunt—the trampoline. Once she was comfortable doing her flip-flops

Trampoline

Competition trampolines are so powerful that they can send gymnasts as high as 30 feet in the air to easily perform such skills as double, triple, and twisting somersaults.

Power Tumbling

Power tumbling is performed on spring runways that help tumblers go higher than a basketball hoop while performing explosive somersaults with multiple flips and twists.

Double Mini-Trampoline

Double mini is a relatively new sport that combines the run of power tumbling with the height of the trampoline. It's a lot like springboard diving—only using a mat instead of water. The gymnast jumps onto a small trampoline to perform a trick followed by a dismount onto a mat.

there, she moved back to the floor. As Rebecca found her groove again, she added the rest of her back handsprings to her routine one at a time until she felt she was ready to compete.

"When I finally overcame the problem, I knew that it was just a lack of confidence. And the harder I concentrated, the better I felt about it," says Rebecca, who made a spectacular turnaround that led to placing first in tumbling at state, second at regionals, and fourth at a national competition.

Freeze Out Fear

When fear puts the freeze on, warm up with these tips:

Identify the fear: Figure out where the fear is coming from so that you know better how to handle it.

Back up and start over: Sometimes fear comes and goes in a flash. Clear your mind and try the stunt again.

Get a spot: Knowing that someone is there to catch you if you fall may be the first step toward going solo again.

Back to basics: Practicing simpler skills you know can boost your confidence and help calm your nerves.

Picture it—fearless: Keep picturing yourself as a fearless person and repeat encouraging words in your mind. You can do anything—and you know it!

Heather

Heather U. hopes to follow in the footsteps of such gymnasts as 2004 Olympic gold medalist Carly Patterson.

Watching gymnasts practice at Heather's gym can be a lot like watching a real Olympic event. That's because Heather attends one of the top girls' gymnastics-training centers in the country. Heather's gymnastics academy trains many top-level gymnasts, such as 2004 Olympic gold medalist Carly Patterson. "I feel fortunate to live where I do so that I can train at such a great gym," says Heather, who loves to watch the gymnasts train, talk to them, and congratulate them after they win big competitions.

The most memorable "well done" that Heather ever gave was to Carly Patterson after she had won the gold medal for all-around in Athens, Greece. "I went to the airport with my teammates to meet Carly,"

remembers Heather. "I had my picture taken with her and asked her to sign it. I look at it daily to keep myself motivated for practices."

Staying motivated can be tricky for some gymnasts, especially when they've practiced the same routine hundreds of times. But in spring 2006, Heather had to find a new form of motivation in order for her and her team to learn four new Level 6 compulsory routines before a meet three months away. "All of my teammates were nervous, especially since we would have to do all new skills on all of the events," says Heather. She got right to work and made the most of the 18 to 20 hours of practice she has each week.

The meet got off to a shaky start on the balance beam when Heather and her teammates each had to perform a back walkover for the first time without being spotted by their coach. "My first teammate fell off during a full turn. That made the rest of us nervous because she never falls off the beam," Heather remembers. The second teammate wobbled but didn't fall. Heather almost fell during her back walkover but saved it. With a 9.475, Heather was excited to receive the highest score on her team.

"I look at this picture daily to keep myself motivated for practices!"

For their first Level 6 competition, Heather and her team did really well. "We all hugged and congratulated each other. It was a great way to start a new season!" says Heather. If she can continue to work hard toward moving up, Heather might just follow in the big footsteps of the top-ranked gymnasts who came before her. "My coaches and teammates are the best," says Heather. "That motivation is what I need to help me develop into the best gymnast I can be."

Gym Fun

Gymnastics isn't all about hard work and skill drills.
Enjoy some friendship and fun along the way!

Games

Turn practice time into fun and you won't even
know you're working on your gymnastics skills!

"I Did It!"

Arrange several hoops on the ground in a big circle (use pillows if you're playing at home). Pile lots of bean-bags or stuffed animals in the center of the circle. Each player gets a hoop to sit in. On "go," everyone runs to the center, grabs a beanie, and puts it in her hoop. The object is to get three beanies in your hoop—but wait, there's a catch!

Players can swipe beanies from one another's hoops, too, so you need a bit of strategy. Once you have three beanies in your hoop, lie down on them and yell, "I did it!"

Play again, but this time players have to crabwalk to the center, put the beanies on their tummies, and crab-walk them to their hoops. Play again balancing beanies on your heads, or try it without using hands!

45

Dance Tag

(You'll need one player, or a coach, to run the music.) Stand in a big circle with your friends or teammates. Turn on dance music. Take turns going into the center of the circle to dance for a couple of minutes. It's easier if a few of you dance in the middle at one time. When the music stops, pick someone else to take your spot in the center. It might feel awkward at first, but it really helps you get comfortable dancing in front of others—which you'll have to do sooner or later if you plan to compete.

Stick It!

One person, such as the coach, is the caller. She calls out a gymnastics jump or skill, starting with something pretty basic, such as a tuck jump. Everyone else does a tuck jump and tries to "stick it" (take no steps on the landing). If someone takes a step on her landing, she's out. The caller calls a skill that's a little more difficult each time. The last person still in is the winner!

Tricks to Stick
Handstand, cartwheel, straight jump–full turn, cartwheel–straddle jump, round-off–straddle jump, and round-off–full turn

Tuck Jump!

Crafts

Save your gymnastics memories and create your very own wall of fame!

Scrapshots

Look for special gymnastics stickers at scrapbook supply stores, and create a colorful scrapbook page of meet memories and photos. Save your page in a scrapbook or frame it and hang it in your room.

Sarah

Name Frame

Get a frame with a large mat and frame your team pic. Have your teammates sign the mat for a special season memento.

Shorts Style

Get your team or gymnastics friends together and create your own practice uniforms. Use fabric paint to personalize matching shorts with your initials, your team name, or a favorite nickname.

Bow-Tie Bear

Attach your meet ribbons to a bow tied around a stuffed animal's neck.

Medal Mania

Display your medals on hooks
that you paint yourself and then
decorate with stickers, if you like.

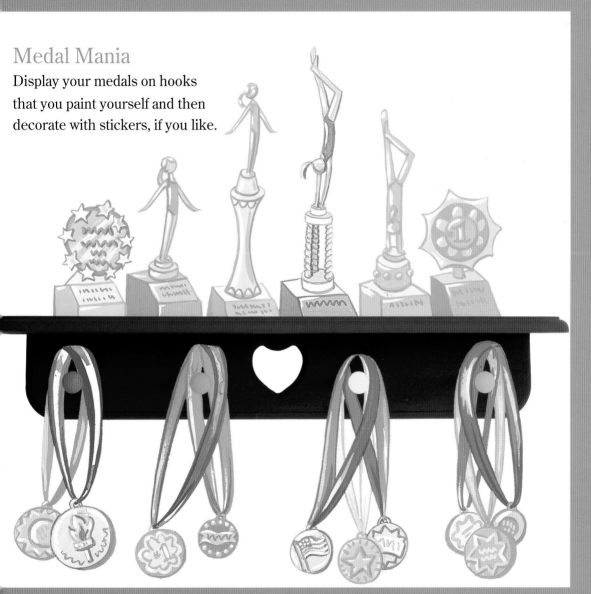

Just 'Do It!

Try these styles to keep your hair neat for meets.

Front Row

1 Separate hair into 6 equal sections, and hold each in place with mini clips.

2 Secure each section with a small pony-o.

3 Gather the rest of your hair into a high ponytail and secure with a scrunchie.

Use extra hair clips and hair spray or hair gel to keep hair in place during a competition.

French Braids

1 Part hair down the back of the head for pigtails. Use an elastic to hold one section off to the side.

2 On the other side, gather hair from the front of the head and separate it into 3 equal sections.

3 Begin by crossing over the sections once, as you would for a regular braid.

4 Grab a few strands of hair to the left of the braid and add to the left-hand section. Cross the section over the center.

5 Grab a few strands of hair to the right of the braid and add to the right-hand section. Cross the section over the center.

6 Repeat until all hair has been added. Then continue with a regular braid. Tie off with an elastic. Repeat on the other side.

Eats & Treats

Try these smoothies and snacks for a delicious way to get your fruit and veggie servings each day!

MENU

The Basic Ingredients:
Most fruit smoothies have three basic ingredients: sliced bananas, frozen fruit, and fruit juice. You also need a blender and some creativity!

Directions:
✋ Put all the ingredients in the blender in the order listed and have an adult mix on high speed until fully blended.

Simple Smoothie
2 bananas
10 to 12 frozen strawberries
1 cup apple juice

Vitamin C-ya!
2 bananas
1 orange
2 kiwis
10 to 12 frozen strawberries
½ cup frozen blueberries
1 to 2 cups orange juice

Go Bananas!

2 bananas
1 apple
1 orange
1 chunk fresh pineapple
1 to 2 cups apple juice

Mighty Melon

2 bananas
¼ cantaloupe
¼ honeydew
1 cup frozen melon chunks
1 cup apple juice

Just Peachy

2 bananas
1 cup frozen peaches
1 cup apple juice

B-O-P to the Top

2 **B**ananas
2 **O**ranges
3 chunks fresh **P**ineapple
10 to 12 frozen strawberries
1 to 2 cups orange juice

Tropical Twist

2 bananas
1 mango
2 kiwis
½ papaya
10 to 12 frozen strawberries
1 to 2 cups cranberry juice

Berry Good

2 bananas
1 cup raspberries
½ cup frozen blueberries
10 to 12 frozen strawberries
1 to 2 cups cranberry juice

Sweet 'n' Sour Apple

2 bananas
1 green apple
1 red apple
10 to 12 frozen strawberries
1 to 2 cups apple juice

Veggie Twisters

4 nine-inch flour tortillas
3 tablespoons softened
  cream cheese (for each twister)
1 small cucumber, sliced
Alfalfa sprouts
Sliced tomato
Salt and pepper

Spread cream cheese on each tortilla. Top
with cucumber and tomato slices and a
small handful of fresh sprouts. Sprinkle
with salt and pepper to taste. Fold in sides
and tightly roll up each tortilla. Slice in
half diagonally. If desired, secure with
wooden toothpicks. Serve right away.

*For another tasty treat packed with
protein, spread peanut butter on a tortilla
and top it with banana slices.*

"Stick It!" Bars

2½ cups crisp rice cereal
2 cups quick-cooking oats
½ cup raisins
½ cup firmly packed brown sugar
½ cup light corn syrup
½ cup peanut butter
1 teaspoon vanilla extract
½ cup semisweet chocolate chips

1 Combine first 3 ingredients in a large bowl; set aside.

2 Have an adult help you bring brown sugar and syrup to a boil in a small saucepan over medium-high heat, stirring constantly; remove from heat. Stir in peanut butter and vanilla until blended.

3 Pour peanut-butter mixture over cereal mixture, stirring until coated; let stand 10 minutes.

4 Stir in chocolate chips. Press mixture into a greased 13-by-9-inch pan; cool in pan on a wire rack.

5 Cut into bars.
Makes 4 dozen.

Meal Matters

It's especially important for athletes like gymnasts to eat right. Burning extra calories means you'll have to make sure your body gets the nourishment it needs. Find foods with calcium for strong bones and protein to provide the energy you'll need to get through those long practices.

Say What?

Learn the lingo of gymnastics skills.

Aerial—a skill without hands, such as a no-hand cartwheel, walkover, or round-off

Arabian—a jump backward with a half turn into a front somersault

Back Handspring—a jump backward onto the hands, followed by a quick push from the hands to the feet (also called flip-flop or flic-flac)

Barani—a front flip with a half twist

Bridge—a position in which the body is curved backward making an arch. Hands and feet are flat on the floor.

Cast Handstand—on bars, a swing up to a handstand either beginning from a front support or transitioning from another skill

Flyaway—a swing forward (usually on the high bar) back to a salto dismount

Flyspring—a forward-moving skill with gymnast taking off on two feet to the hands, followed by a quick push from the hands to two feet

Front Limber—a forward skill with gymnast moving from a handstand to a bridge to a standing position

Front through to Back—a tumbling pass that begins with a punch front and ends with a back somersault

Full—a back somersault with a twist. A *full-in* is a double back salto with a full twist during the first salto. A *full-out* is a double back salto with a full twist during the second salto.

Giant—a swing in which the body is fully extended and moving through a 360-degree rotation around the bar

Half-In—a double back salto with a half twist on the first salto. A *half-out* is a double back salto with a half twist on the second salto.

Handspring—springing from the feet to the hands to the feet again. It is used as its own skill or as a linking skill and can be done forward or backward.

Kip—a bar movement in which the gymnast first *pikes* and then forcefully extends the body outward to finish in a support on the bar

Layout—a salto performed in a stretched body position, straight or slightly arched

Pike—a position in which the body is bent more than 90 degrees at the hips while straight legs are maintained

Pirouette—a turn, usually when turning on one foot or in a handstand

Punch Front—a front salto with takeoff from two feet

Randy—a front flip with two and a half twists

Round-off—a turning movement, with a push-off onto one leg while swinging the legs upward in a fast cartwheel to a 90-degree turn

Rudi—a front flip with one and a half twists

Salto—flip or somersault, with the feet coming up over the head and the body rotating around the axis of the waist (without hands)

Shushunova—straddle jump on floor landing on stomach

Somersault—any movement in which the gymnast flips and rotates in a complete circle in the air (also called somi, sommie)

Splits—a position in which the legs are extended apart, making a straight line. Middle or straddle splits are done with the body facing forward and the legs extending to the sides. Left splits are done with the left leg forward and the right leg extended back. Right splits are done with the right leg forward and the left leg extended back.

Straddle—a position used in leaps and jumps in which the legs are extended apart to the sides while the hips remain centered. Straddle jumps and leaps for high-level gymnasts should be at or over 180 degrees (a full split).

Tuck—a forward or back somersault in the tuck position

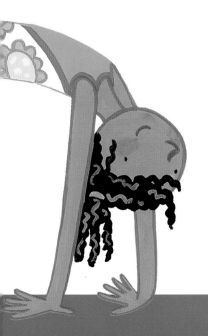

Tuck Position—hips are bent at more than 90 degrees with legs completely bent and knees touching chest

Twist—flip or somersault, with the feet coming up over the head and the body rotating side to side

Walkover—move with gymnast beginning on leg moving through a bridge position to end on one foot with legs remaining split throughout the skill. This skill can be done forward or backward.

Whip—no-handed back handspring used to generate power and speed into another skill

Wolf jump—a pike jump with one leg bent tightly and knees kept together

Yurchenko—a vault performed with a round-off entry onto the springboard

Here are some other American Girl books you might like:

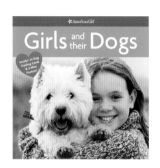

❑ I read it.

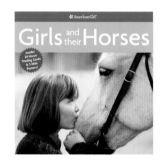

❑ I read it.

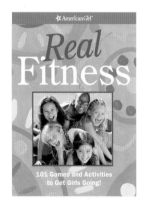

❑ I read it.

❑ I read it.

I flip

for gymnastics!

salute!

☆ American Girl®

Gymnastics makes my heart soar.

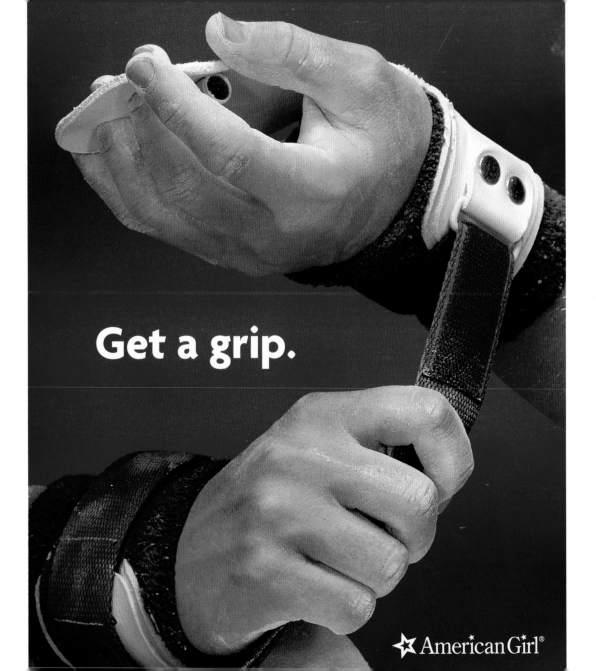

Get a grip.

★ American Girl®